BEYOND DINOSAURS! My First Book About UNDERWATER CREATURES

For you, Richard Carr. I finally wrote something about fish.

Interior and Cover Designer: Gabe Nansen
Art Producer: Janice Ackerman
Editor: Annie Choi
Associate Editor: Maxine Marshall

[Photography/Illustrations © Artist name, year] Design note: use for stand-alone custom photo/illustration credit

ISBN: Print 978-1-64611-935-6 | eBook 978-1-64611-936-3

R0

BEYOND DINOSAURS! My First Book About UNDERWATER CREATURES

By Cary Woodruff

Illustrations by Annalisa & Marina Durante

ROCKRIDGE PRESS

ALL ABOUT THE PREHISTORIC SEAS!

A very long time ago, the seas were filled with swimming **prehistoric** creatures. In fact, the first animals on Earth lived in the water.

We learn everything that we know about prehistoric creatures from **fossils**. **Paleontologists** are the scientists who dig up and study the fossils of prehistoric plants and animals. Thanks to fossils, we know which prehistoric animals could swim, what they ate, and how long ago they lived.

Before animals could walk on land, they swam in water. All land animals **evolved** from ancient fish, like coelacanths (SEE-low-can-th) and *Tiktaalik* (tick-TAH-lick), creatures that you'll see in this book. Some swimming creatures, like fish and sharks, lived 300 million years before the first dinosaur ever appeared!

Although we know a lot about swimming prehistoric animals, scientists are always making new discoveries and learning new things. Maybe one day you will help scientists discover another ancient swimming creature!

*The **evolution** of arms like yours began with the fins of a fish years ago. These fins were made of one large bone that connected to two smaller bones (just like your arms!). Those bones then connected to many tiny bones, like your fingers.*

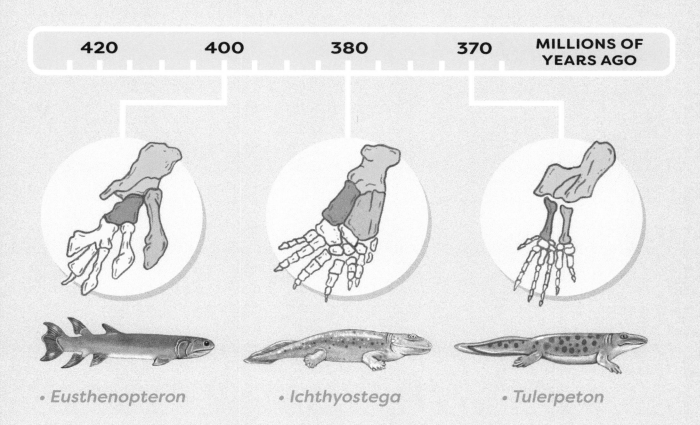

| 420 | 400 | 380 | 370 | MILLIONS OF YEARS AGO |

• *Eusthenopteron*   • *Ichthyostega*   • *Tulerpeton*

PREHISTORIC TIME

In this book, you'll learn about 30 amazing creatures, from spiral-shelled ammonites (AH-mo-night) to the largest **marine** reptile ever—the 69-foot-long *Shastasaurus*. All these creatures lived on Earth during different time periods.

CAMBRIAN PERIOD

From 541 to 485 million years ago. At the beginning of this period, there was a big "explosion" of life, when many of Earth's animals first evolved.

DEVONIAN PERIOD

From 419 to 358 million years ago. Also known as the "Age of Fishes."

TRIASSIC PERIOD

From 251 to 201 million years ago. Pterosaurs (TER-a-SORS) and dinosaurs first evolved during this period.

CAMBRIAN	DEVONIAN	MISSISSIPPIAN	PERMIAN	TRIASSIC	JURASSIC	CRETACEO...
PALEOZOIC ERA				**MESOZOIC ERA**		

JURASSIC PERIOD

From 201 to 145 million years ago. Also known as the "Age of Giants." Some of the largest dinosaurs lived during this period. It's also when birds, a group of dinosaurs, first appeared.

CRETACEOUS PERIOD

From 145 to 66 million years ago. This is when some famous dinosaurs, like the *Triceratops* and *Tyrannosaurus,* lived. At the end of this period, all dinosaurs except birds became **extinct** when an asteroid hit Earth.

CENOZOIC ERA

From 66 million years ago through today. Also known as the "Age of Mammals."

ALEOCENE EOCENE OLIGOCENE MIOCENE PLIOCENE PLEISTOCENE HOLOCENE

CENOZOIC ERA

Haikouichthys means "Haikou fish." Haikou is the name of a city in China where the fossil was first discovered.

HAIKOUICHTHYS

SAY IT! hi-KOO-ick-these / **TYPE:** Early chordate

Haikouichthys lived during the Cambrian period, when lots of creatures appeared in a short amount of time. Scientists call this time the "Cambrian Explosion." *Haikouichthys* was not a **vertebrate** like us. Instead, *Haikouichthys* belongs to a group called **chordates**. It had a head and tail, muscles, a spinal cord, and gills, but no jaw or skeleton. All vertebrates—fish, reptiles, dinosaurs, and mammals (including us!)—evolved from chordates.

Thousands of *Haikouichthys* fossils have been found together in sites that preserve their **soft tissues,** like skin and muscles.

Length: 1 inch

When: Early Cambrian Period—535 to 520 million years ago

Where: China

It ate: plankton

It was the size of: an eraser

AMMONITE

SAY IT! **AH-mo-night** / TYPE: **Invertebrate**

Imagine a creature with the body of a squid inside the shell of a snail—that's what many ammonites looked like. Ammonites were **invertebrates** that swam throughout all of Earth's prehistoric oceans. Even though they had shells, they were related to squids and octopuses. Most ammonites had spiral-shaped shells, but others had shells with different shapes like coiled springs or straight lines.

Shell size: from 1 inch to 6 feet

When: Early Devonian to Late Cretaceous Periods— 409 to 66 million years ago

Where: oceans all over the world

It ate: plankton or fish

It was as long as: an adult human

Ammonite shells are covered in zigzag patterns. These zigzags helped connect parts of the shell together.

Paleontologists have discovered over 10,000 **species** of ammonites!

PALEOZOIC ERA   MESOZOIC ERA   CENOZOIC ERA

Paleontologists first thought coelacanths went extinct 66 million years ago, but then living coelacanths were found off the east coast of Africa in 1938!

COELACANTH

The special fins on a coelacanth are called "lobed" fins. Most other fish have fins made of long, skinny bones arranged like a fan. The fins on a coelacanth have one big bone at the top connecting to two smaller bones, and many thin, small bones at the tip. This is just like the bones in your arms and legs, and the limbs on other mammals. The first land animals with arms and legs evolved from fish like the coelacanth.

Length: from a few inches to 11 feet

When: Late Devonian Period to present— 409 million years ago to today

Where: oceans all over the world

It ate: squid, octopus, and other fish

It was the size of: a minnow, up to the size of a giant sturgeon fish

Coelacanths don't lay eggs like other fish. They give birth to live young.

PALEOZOIC ERA   MESOZOIC ERA   CENOZOIC ERA

DUNKLEOSTEUS

The mighty *Dunkleosteus* belonged to a group of fish called **placoderms**. The head and jaws of *Dunkleosteus* were protected by plates of bone **armor**, making them very strong. Instead of teeth, it had sharp, pointy bits of bone sticking out of its mouth. *Dunkleosteus* was a great **predator**. *Dunkleosteus* had strong jaws and could bite through other armored fish—it may have eaten other *Dunkleosteus* as well.

Length: up to 20 feet

When: Late Devonian Period—382 to 358 million years ago

Where: North America, Poland, Belgium, Morocco, and Australia

It ate: ammonites and other fish

It was the size of: a killer whale

Tiktaalik may have stuck its head out of the water to breathe. It might have even stood on land for short amounts of time.

TIKTAALIK

Tiktaalik is a very important fossil for learning about the evolution of life on land. It is a **transitional fossil** that shows how land animals evolved from fish. Just like coelacanths, *Tiktaalik* had lobed fins. But the fins of *Tiktaalik* were even more arm-like. *Tiktaalik* had shoulder bones, so scientists know that its fins supported its body weight, just like our legs do when we stand. *Tiktaalik* probably walked along the edge of the water to hunt.

Size: up to 9 feet

When: Late Devonian Period—375 million years ago

Where: Canada

It ate: other fish and insects

It was as long as: a basketball hoop

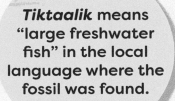

Tiktaalik means "large freshwater fish" in the local language where the fossil was found.

CRASSIGYRINUS

Crassigyrinus was a very strange **amphibian**. It had a long body, a giant square-shaped head, and four tiny legs. Its legs were so small that they could not support its own weight. It lived its entire life swimming in the water. *Crassigyrinus* had large eyes to help it see better while it chased and caught prey in murky swamps.

The name *Crassigyrinus* means "thick tadpole." Do you think it looks like a tadpole?

The first *Crassigyrinus* fossils were found in Scotland.

Size: 6.5 feet

When: Middle Mississippian Period—345 to 328 million years ago

Where: Europe

It ate: fish

It was as long as: an adult human

PALEOZOIC ERA   MESOZOIC ERA   CENOZOIC ERA

Because so many fish have been found in the Bear Gulch Limestone, scientists think it was a place where fish came to give birth.

FALCATUS

SAY IT! fal-KAY-tuss
TYPE: Fish

Length: 1 foot

When: Upper Mississippian Period—328 to 318 million years ago

Where: United States

It ate: other fish

It was the size of: a ruler

ECHINOCHIMAERA

SAY IT! ee-KEY-no-ka-MARE-ah
TYPE: Fish

Length: 6 inches

When: Upper Mississippian Period—328 to 318 million years ago

Where: United States

It ate: shellfish

It was the size of: a pencil

Falcatus and *Echinochimaera* fossils were both discovered in the Bear Gulch Limestone deposit in Montana. The Bear Gulch Limestone is famous because scientists have found lots of fish fossils there. Many of these fossils include not only bone but also preserved soft tissues like skin and scales.

Falcatus was an odd little shark. The males had a hook-like spine on the top of their heads, but females did not. *Echinochimaera* was also a very strange fish, but instead of spines on top of their heads, male *Echinochimaera* had four pairs of spines on their fins.

The tooth whorl did not spin, but it did change the way *Helicoprion* could move its jaws. Imagine trying to move your mouth with a tooth whorl inside!

HELICOPRION

Helicoprion had very special teeth. Its teeth grew in a spiral in its mouth, like a saw blade. Paleontologists call this a **tooth whorl**. For a long time, paleontologists did not know what part of the body the tooth whorl attached to. At first, they thought the tooth whorl was attached to the tip of the snout like a spiraled, toothy nose. Some paleontologists also thought that maybe it was attached to one of the fins. But now, paleontologists believe the tooth whorl was inside the mouth.

Helicoprion is often called the "buzzsaw shark" because of its tooth whorl.

Length: up to 39 feet

When: Permian Period—290 million years ago

Where: North America, Europe, Asia, and Australia

It ate: other fish

It was the size of: a school bus

Atopodentatus means "strange tooth" because of its odd teeth and the shape of its snout.

ATOPODENTATUS

Atopodentatus had a snout shaped like a vacuum cleaner. This wide snout helped *Atopodentatus* graze and feed on tiny algae on the sea floor. Almost all other marine reptiles are predators that eat fish, squid, or even each other. Scientists know of only two marine reptiles that did not eat meat. *Atopodentatus* was perhaps one of the very first marine reptiles that was an **herbivore**.

The first *Atopodentatus* fossil ever found was damaged. This made paleontologists think that *Atopodentatus* could open its mouth to the left and right, in addition to up and down!

Length: almost 10 feet

When: Middle Triassic Period—245 to 228 million years ago

Where: China

It ate: algae

It was the size of: a lion

TANYSTROPHEUS

Tanystropheus had a very long neck—it was longer than the whole rest of its body. Paleontologists think *Tanystropheus* used its long neck to reach out and snatch fish. *Tanystropheus* might have hunted by swimming or walking in shallow water to sneak up on fish. Or it may have stood at the edge of the water and grabbed fish from above, just like a heron.

Length: 20 feet

When: Middle Triassic Period—245 to 228 million years ago

Where: Germany, Italy, and China

It ate: fish

It was the size of: a car

Tanystropheus' long neck is made of 13 bones. A human neck has only 7.

PALEOZOIC ERA   MESOZOIC ERA   CENOZOIC ERA

One of the first *Tanystropheus* fossils found was mistakenly identified as a pterosaur. Scientists thought that it flew instead of swam!

SHASTASAURUS

SAY IT! SHAZ-tah-SORE-us / **TYPE:** Marine reptile

Shastasaurus is the largest marine reptile ever discovered! Just like whale sharks that swim in the ocean today, *Shastasaurus* was a gentle giant. *Shastasaurus* swam slowly, powered by four large paddles. *Shastasaurus* had a short snout and no teeth, which means that it probably swallowed its prey whole.

Length: up to 70 feet

When: Middle to Late Triassic Period—235 to 205 million years ago

Where: North America and China

It ate: squid

It was the size of: an oak tree

You can see a nearly complete skeleton of *Shastasaurus* at the Royal Tyrell Museum in Alberta, Canada.

Shastasaurus means "Mt. Shasta lizard" because the first fossil was found near Mt. Shasta in California.

HENODUS

With its arms, legs, tail, and head coming out of a shell, you may think that *Henodus* was a turtle. But it was not! *Henodus* looks like a turtle because of **convergent evolution**— the two creatures both have shells because shells are helpful protection from predators. But the shell of *Henodus* and a turtle's shell are very different. On a turtle, most of the shell is made from the turtle's rib bones. But on *Henodus*, the shell is made of many pieces of bone that stick to the outside of the skeleton and fit together like a puzzle.

Length: 3 feet

When: Late Triassic Period— 228 to 220 million years ago

Where: Germany

It ate: aquatic plants

It was the size of: a dog

Henodus belonged to a group of marine reptiles called the placodonts, which means "tablet teeth" because their teeth are flat and box shaped.

Ichthyosaurus had big eyes to see well in dark water.

Ichthyosaurus means "fish lizard."

ICHTHYOSAURUS

Ichthyosaurus was the very first marine reptile ever discovered, and it was collected by Mary Anning, the world's first female paleontologist. *Ichthyosaurus* looked like a fish, but we know it was a reptile because of its teeth, the bones in its flippers, and special holes in its skull. *Ichthyosaurus* has a body that looks like a fish because that is the best body shape for moving in water. This is the same reason why dolphins and sharks also have similar bodies.

The first *Ichthyosaurus* fossils were found in Lyme Regis, England. Many marine fossils are still being discovered there today.

Length: up to 11 feet

When: Early Jurassic Period—199 to 190 million years ago

Where: Europe

It ate: fish and squid

It was the size of: two horses put together

LEEDSICHTHYS

Leedsichthys was very large, but it wasn't a scary predator. It was actually very gentle. As it swam through the ocean, *Leedsichthys* kept its mouth open to catch tiny plants and animals called plankton using special bones in the back of its mouth called **gill rakers**. Whale sharks—the largest fish alive today—catch plankton in exactly the same way. Unlike whale sharks, though, *Leedsichthys* had a skeleton made of bone instead of **cartilage**.

Length: up to 54 feet

When: Middle Jurassic Period—165 to 152 million years ago

Where: Europe and South America

It ate: plankton

It was the size of: two school busses end to end

The first *Leedsichthys* fossil was found in England. When it was first found, scientists mistakenly thought it was parts from a dinosaur.

Leedsichthys was the largest fish with a bony skeleton.

PALEOZOIC ERA   MESOZOIC ERA   CENOZOIC ERA

PLIOSAURUS

Pliosaurus was a top predator in the ancient ocean. With teeth that were 12 inches long, *Pliosaurus* was always on the hunt for its next meal. Powered by four large flippers, it could quickly chase down prey. *Pliosaurus* is part of a group of reptiles called the pliosaurs (PLY-oh-sores). The bodies of pliosaurs and another group of reptiles called plesiosaurs (PLEASE-ee-oh-sores), looked very similar: They both had round bodies, short tails, and four flippers for swimming. But plesiosaurs had extremely long necks, while pliosaurs, like *Pliosaurus*, had very short necks.

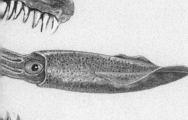

Pliosaurus had a skull that was over eight feet long.

Size: 49 feet

When: Late Jurassic Period—155 to 147 million years ago

Where: South America and Europe

It ate: large fish, other marine reptiles, and dinosaurs

It was longer than: a *Tyrannosaurus rex*

DAKOSAURUS

SAY IT! DAH-ko-SORE-us / **TYPE:** Marine reptile

Dakosaurus belonged to a special group of marine crocodiles that lived their entire lives in the sea and gave birth to their babies in the ocean as well. *Dakosaurus* had four short flippers. It used these flippers, along with a powerful tail, to ambush and catch prey. *Dakosaurus* ate its prey with big sharp teeth that were shaped like steak knives, perfect for biting and eating meat.

Too much salt is a problem for marine animals. Like marine animals today, the skull of *Dakosaurus* has space to store and remove extra salt from ocean water.

Size: 15 feet

When: Late Jurassic to Early Cretaceous Periods— 157 to 137 million years ago

Where: Europe and South America

It ate: large fish and other marine reptiles

It was as long as: a soccer goal post

PALEOZOIC ERA   MESOZOIC ERA   CENOZOIC ERA

Dakosaurus means "biter lizard" because of its big teeth.

XIPHACTINUS

Xiphactinus was a large predator that lived in the ancient seas during the time of the dinosaurs. *Xiphactinus* may have lived and traveled in schools, just like many fish do today. *Xiphactinus* had a big appetite. One famous fossil found in the 1950s was a 13-foot *Xiphactinus* with a 6-foot-long fish stuck inside of it! The *Xiphactinus* likely choked from trying to eat a fish that was too big.

Xiphactinus fossils were found in Kansas. During the Cretaceous period, there was an ocean in the middle of North America.

Length: up to 20 feet

When: Early to Late Cretaceous Period—112 to 66 million years ago

Where: North and South America, Europe, and Australia

It ate: other fish

It was the size of: a giraffe

PALEOZOIC ERA   MESOZOIC ERA   CENOZOIC ERA

Xiphactinus may have weighed nearly 1,000 pounds. That's heavier than a grand piano.

DEINOSUCHUS

SAY IT! die-no-SUE-cuss
TYPE: Reptile

Deinosuchus was one of the largest crocodilians to ever live. *Deinosuchus* likely caught and fed upon unsuspecting dinosaurs. Just like crocodiles and alligators today, *Deinosuchus* was an ambush predator, waiting at the water's edge to snatch prey when it came for a drink.

Size: 35 feet

When: Late Cretaceous Period—82 to 73 million years ago

Where: North America

It ate: fish, other reptiles, and dinosaurs

It was longer than: a school bus

These two creatures did not live together, but they have a lot in common. Both were similar to modern reptiles, except much, much larger.

40

TITANOBOA

Size: 42 feet

When: Middle to Late Paleocene Period—60 to 58 million years ago

Where: South America

It ate: fish and other reptiles, like crocodilians

It was as long as: a semitruck

Another giant, ancient reptile was *Titanoboa*—the largest snake that ever lived. *Titanoboa* lived in a large tropical swamp. Just like modern pythons and boas, *Titanoboa* was a constrictor. This means that it wrapped its body around its prey and squeezed until the animal could no longer breathe. *Titanoboa* would then swallow its prey whole, in one big gulp.

Titanoboa means "titanic boa," because this snake was so gigantic. *Deinosuchus* means "terrible crocodile."

41

ARCHELON

Archelon swam in the Western Interior Seaway—a warm, shallow ocean that used to be in the middle of North America. It was the largest sea turtle that ever lived. Its shell was as big as a dinner table! While *Archelon*'s body and shell looked a lot like the giant sea turtles alive today, its head was different. *Archelon* had a curved beak that looked almost like a parrot's beak.

Length: 15 feet

When: Late Cretaceous Period—80 to 74 million years ago

Where: North America

It ate: squid and jellyfish

It was the size of: a car

Archelon probably went extinct when the Western Interior Seaway began to dry up.

Archelon means "first turtle" because it was the first sea turtle fossil ever discovered.

ELASMOSAURUS

SAY IT! e-lass-mo-SORE-us
TYPE: Marine reptile

Both *Elasmosaurus* and *Albertonectes* are plesiosaurs (PLEASE-ee-o-sores), a type of creature that swam in the ocean and had extremely long necks. The neck of *Elasmosaurus* was over 20 feet long! We can tell how long the plesiosaurs' necks were by how many bones are used to make them up. Human necks are made of 7 bones, but the neck of *Albertonectes* had 75 bones! Using their four strong flippers, *Elasmosaurus* and *Albertonecte* were very fast swimmers. The plesiosaurs used their long necks to hunt by sneaking up on large groups of fish.

Size: 34 feet

When: Late Cretaceous Period—80 to 72 million years ago

Where: North America

It ate: fish

It was as long as: a city bus

Many marine reptiles—including the plesiosaurs—and all non-bird dinosaurs went extinct around 66 million years ago.

ALBERTONECTES

SAY IT! al-burt-oh-NECK-tees
TYPE: Marine reptile

Size: 38 feet

When: Late Cretaceous Period—80 to 72 million years ago

Where: North America

It ate: fish

It was as long as: a *Tyrannosaurus rex*

When the first *Elasmosaurus* fossil was found, the discoverer put the head on the wrong end! He thought *Elasmosaurus* had a short neck and a long tail!

MOSASAURUS

Mosasaurus was the top predator in the Western Interior Seaway. With its 5-foot-long skull filled with sharp teeth, few animals were safe from an attacking *Mosasaurus*. But the inside of a *Mosasaurus* mouth was extra scary—it had a second set of teeth inside its mouth called **palatal teeth**. Snakes have palatal teeth as well. So, some paleontologists thought that *Mosasaurus* evolved from marine snakes. Many now think that they are more similar to monitor lizards like the Komodo dragon.

Size: 56 feet

When: Late Cretaceous Period—70 to 66 million years ago

Where: Europe and North America

It ate: large fish, other marine reptiles, ammonites, and even dinosaurs

It was as long as: a fighter jet

Mosasaurus may have been dark on top of its body, and lighter underneath, just like great white sharks, orcas, and many other marine predators today.

PALEOZOIC ERA | MESOZOIC ERA | CENOZOIC ERA

Ammonite shells have been found with *Mosasaurus* tooth marks on them. Imagine how sharp your teeth would need to be to bite through a seashell!

Unlike modern whales, *Basilosaurus* chewed its food.

BASILOSAURUS

SAY IT! BA-sill-o-SORE-us / **TYPE:** Mammal

Basilosaurus may look like a snake or eel, but it was actually an early whale. The skull of *Basilosaurus* is asymmetrical—this means that the left and right sides of its head are shaped differently. Modern whales have similar asymmetric skulls which help them **echolocate**, so paleontologists think that *Basilosaurus* used an early form of echolocation to find its way around.

In the desert in Egypt, you can see *Basilosaurus* fossil skeletons lying in the ground. This famous location is called Wadi Al-Hitan (WHA-dee all he-TANN).

Size: up to 66 feet

When: Late Eocene Period—41 to 33 million years ago

Where: North America and Africa

It ate: fish, sharks, and other whales

It was as long as: two city buses

OTODUS

Otodus was the largest predatory shark of all time. You may have heard about *Otodus* by its other name, *megalodon*. In science, plants and animals have two-part names, like *Tyrannosaurus rex*, *Boa constrictor*, or *Homo sapiens* (that's the **scientific name** for humans!). This ancient shark's scientific name is *Otodus megalodon*. We don't normally refer to animals by the second part of their name, but this famous shark is an exception. *Otodus* was very big and had a giant appetite to match. Paleontologists have discovered several whale fossils that are covered with the bite marks from *Otodus*.

Size: almost 60 feet

When: Miocene to Pliocene Periods—23 to 3 million years ago

Where: North and South America, Europe, Asia, Africa, and Australia

It ate: whales, dolphins, seals, and sea turtles

It was as long as: two fire trucks

The biggest *Otodus* tooth ever found is seven inches long.

PALEOZOIC ERA   MESOZOIC ERA   CENOZOIC ERA

STUPENDEMYS

Stupendemys was the largest freshwater turtle. It lived in a giant wetland that covered the top half of South America. But *Stupendemys* wasn't the only giant in this ecosystem—it lived alongside the giant crocodile-type creature *Purussaurus* (pure-RAH-sore-us) and the giant rodent *Phoberomys* (fo-BEAR-oh-meez).

Stupendemys' heavy shell helped it stay underwater as it slowly swam along. The male *Stupendemys* had a small horn on each side of its shell. They probably used these horns to fight each other, something many turtles do today.

Stupendemys means "stupendous turtle" because of its giant size.

Size: 11 feet

When: Late Miocene to Early Pliocene Periods—13 to 5 million years ago

Where: South America

It ate: fish, shellfish, and aquatic plants

It was as long as: a Jet Ski

PALEOZOIC ERA   MESOZOIC ERA   CENOZOIC ERA

Stupendemys geographicus is named in honor of the 1972 National Geographic Society expedition that found the first *Stupendemys* fossils.

Giant bears used to catch and eat *Oncorhynchus*, just like grizzly bears feed on salmon today.

ONCORHYNCHUS

SAY IT! **ON-ko-RINK-us** / TYPE: **Fish**

Oncorhynchus is related to the salmon and trout that swim in our rivers today. Some kinds of *Oncorhynchus* had two long, pointy teeth sticking out of their mouths. These teeth gave this fish its nickname, the "saber-toothed salmon." *Oncorhynchus* did not use these scary teeth to catch prey—it filtered plankton, just like *Leedsichthys* (see page 32). Instead, the fish may have used its saber-shaped teeth to defend itself or compete with other fish.

New fossils of *Oncorhynchus* show that its saber-shaped teeth may have pointed down.

Size: 9 feet

When: Early Pliocene Period—12 to 5 million years ago

Where: North America

It ate: plankton

It was longer than: a professional basketball player

LIVYATAN

With a 10-foot-long skull, *Livyatan* is the largest whale with teeth ever discovered. *Livyatan* is related to the modern sperm whale, but *Livyatan* had huge, banana-size teeth on its upper and lower jaws. Today, the sperm whale dives deep in the ocean to hunt giant squids. But paleontologists think that *Livyatan* probably hunted other whales near the water's surface. *Livyatan* also lived alongside the giant shark *Otodus megalodon*. Did *Livyatan* and *Otodus* compete for food? It is fascinating to wonder how two giant predators lived together in the same ecosystem.

The name *Livyatan* refers to the biblical monster Leviathan.

Size: up to 57 feet

When: Miocene Period—9 to 8 million years ago

Where: South America

It ate: other whales and marine vertebrates

It was as long as: a semitruck

PALEOZOIC ERA   MESOZOIC ERA   CENOZOIC ERA

Livyatan's species name is *melvillei*, in honor of Herman Melville, the author of *Moby-Dick*, a famous story about a large, white sperm whale that attacks ships.

ODOBENOCETOPS

Odobenocetops is sometimes called the "walrus whale," and it's easy to see why—it had a box-shaped head, a slanted snout, and long tusks, just like a walrus. The strange thing about *Odobenocetops'* tusks is that one was much longer than the other. Paleontologists think that female *Odobenocetops* had two small, similar-sized tusks, and that males had just one long tusk. Did males use their long tusks to fight? We don't know, but mysteries like this make these animals even more fascinating to study.

Odobenocetops is closely related to dolphins.

Length: up to 7 feet

When: Late Miocene to Early Pliocene Periods— 7 to 3 million years ago

Where: South America

It ate: shellfish

It was the size of: an adult human

PALEOZOIC ERA   MESOZOIC ERA   CENOZOIC ERA

Glossary

amphibian: A cold-blooded vertebrate without scales that typically has young that live in the water. Its eggs do not have shells and are laid in water.

armor: Hard protection on the outside of an animal's body. Just like knights wear suits of armor to protect themselves, many animals evolved bony coverings for protection.

aquatic: A plant or animal that lives in water.

cartilage: Tissue that makes up a human nose and ears. Cartilage is softer and more flexible than keratin or bone, but still provides support and shape for body parts.

chordates: A group of animals that vertebrates evolved from. Chordates have a head and tail, muscles, a spinal cord, and gills, but no jaw and no skeleton.

convergent evolution: When plants or animals look similar but are not related. For example, a shark and a dolphin are similarly shaped because they both swim in the ocean, not because they are closely related.

echolocate: "Seeing" with sound. Bats, whales, and dolphins make high-pitched sounds that create a picture of what's around them. It's nature's version of sonar.

evolution: The way all plants and animals change over time. Through multiple generations, small changes add up and cause a new species to be different from the old one.

evolved: To have changed over time, starting with something simple and changing into something more complex.

extinct: Having died out and completely disappeared, as with plants and animals that used to live on Earth.

fossils: The remains of plants and animals that have slowly been turned to stone by minerals in the ground.

gill rakers: Small pieces of bone in the back of some fish mouths. These fish, like whale sharks, swim with their mouths open and use their gill rakers to catch tiny plants and animals.

herbivore: An animal that eats mostly plants.

invertebrate: An animal without internal bones or skeleton.

marine: Living in the ocean.

palatal teeth: A second set of teeth inside the mouth on the palate (PAL-lit) bone. Snakes and *Mosasaurus* have palatal teeth.

paleontologists: Scientists who study fossils to learn about the plants and animals that used to live on Earth.

...nored fish like *Dunkleosteus*. These fish had big,

...animal that hunts other animals for food.

...ric: The time before written history.

...entific name: The name that scientists use for a plant or animal. Scientific names have two parts: the first name is for the group that the plant or animal belongs to, and the second name identifies the particular species.

soft tissue: Skin, muscles, and organs. Soft tissues rarely fossilize.

species: A group of the same animal that can produce babies.

tooth whorl: Teeth that are arranged in a spiral-like pattern.

transitional fossil: A fossil that has traits common to both creatures that lived before it and creatures that lived after it.

vertebrate: An animal with bones.

Index

Placoderms, 12–13

Placodonts, 28

Plesiosaurs, 44–45

Pliosaurus, 34–35

Pterosaurs, 4

Purussaurus, 52

S

Scientific names, 51

Shastasaurus, 4, 26–27

Stupendemys, 52–53

T

Tanystropheus, 24–25

Tiktaalik, 2, 14–15

Titanoboa, 41

Tooth whorls, 21

Transitional fossils, 15

Triassic period, 4

Tulerpeton, 3

V

Vertebrates, 7

W

Wadi Al-Hitan, 49

X

Xiphactinus, 38–39

About the Author

Cary Woodruff grew up in rural central Virginia and received his bachelor's and master's degrees at Montana State University under famed dinosaur paleontologist Dr. Jack Horner. Currently, Cary is the Director of Paleontology at the Great Plains Dinosaur Museum in Malta, Montana. Cary is also a doctoral student at the University of Toronto under Dr. David Evans. Cary specializes in sauropod dinosaurs. His pioneering studies on sauropod growth are changing our understanding of the lives of the biggest animals to ever walk on Earth. Cary has also published research on the first burrowing dinosaur, modern cow vertebral anatomy, dinosaur vision, stegosaurs, and fossil manatees in ancient Egyptian catacombs.

About the Illustrators

Annalisa and **Marina Durante** are nature and science illustrators. They are twin sisters who have loved nature and animals since they were children. Marina enjoys hiking, deep-water diving, and photography. The photos she takes while exploring nature are the inspiration for her art. Annalisa is inspired by Eastern philosophy and enjoys meditating as she explores the outdoors. In 2001, Marina and Annalisa were invited by the Galapagos National Park to draw the birds of the Galapagos Islands. They have worked for the Food and Agriculture Organization (FAO) of the United Nations, illustrating recently discovered species of fish. Their works have been published all over the world, and they have won a number of international art prizes. They especially enjoy illustrating portraits of animals and pets. Find them online at www.duranteillustrations.com.

CPSIA information can be obtained
at www.ICGtesting.com
Printed in the USA
LVHW071510250720
661527LV00004B/11

9 781646 119356